THE
COVERED WAGON
WAY

My Journeys
Across the American Frontier

THE COVERED WAGON WAY

My Journeys Across the American Frontier

May Howe Beardslee

Weddon Press
4891 Dexter Trail
Stockbridge, MI 49285

The COVERED WAGON WAY

Cover illustration and design
by
Hile Illustration and Design

Copyright © 1997 by May Howe Beardslee. All rights reserved.

No part of this book may be reproduced or transmitted in any form or by any means, electronic or mechanical, including photocopying, recording, or by any information storage and retrieval systems, without permission in writing from the co-publisher, except in case of brief quotations embodied in articles and reviews.

Published 1997
First Edition

Published by Weddon Press
4891 Dexter Trail
Stockbridge, MI 49285

Co-publisher: Beverly Beardslee Jackson
1219 Garfield Dr.
Lansing, MI 48917

ISBN 0-9638376-4-8

Library of Congress card number: 94-12045

DEDICATED TO MY THREE DAUGHTERS:

LILLIAN, BEVERLY AND JOYCE,

WHO OFTEN REMINISCED WITH ME.

Table of Contents

PREFACE 1

1 - MICHIGAN FAMILY BACKGROUND 3

2 - TO CALIFORNIA BY COVERED WAGON 6

3 - COOKING ALONG THE TRAIL 10

4 - OUR SECOND TRIP TO CALIFORNIA 16

5 - LIVING IN CALIFORNIA 22

6 - HEADING BACK TO MICHIGAN 27

7 - LIFE IN ONAWAY 31

8 - ON TO OWOSSO AND LANSING 37

••• FAMILY PHOTO SECTION •••

APPENDIX

FRANKIE HOWE'S LETTERS AND RECOLLECTIONS 43

HOWE FAMILY 53

SAMUEL B. SPENCER 59

SPENCER FAMILY 61

PREFACE

When she was little more than four years old, May Castella Howe (Beardslee) left with her family by covered wagon from Michigan for California. The year was 1910. There were seven members in the party: May's parents, her baby sister, her maternal grandparents and their son. The trip across the continent by railroad would have been very expensive for all of them, so they headed out on their own.

Like many other families who had looked to California as the promised land and were disappointed, they returned to Michigan. Unlike other families, they reconsidered and soon made another trip to California…this time with May's paternal grandparents and their four youngest children. Her father was their eldest son. A year later they again returned to Michigan, the covered wagon way.

By now the massive movement to the west, in the late 1800s, had slowed to a trickle. But the trails were well defined, if rugged and rough, and some adventurous souls were still making the long trip by covered wagon. May jotted down notes for more than 30 years about her experiences. Her notes have been compiled into this book. At age 90, she recalls, "What a time in my life it was."

1
MICHIGAN FAMILY BACKGROUND

My parents were living in the village of Corunna, Michigan, when I was born on March 19, 1906. They had been married in Flint, which was about 30 miles east of Corunna, where their families lived. Automobiles were not in use then and it was a long distance to travel with a horse and buggy.

My mother, Estella Maude Spencer Howe, was the only daughter in her family and was lonely without her parents nearby. She had another child, Eliza Adell, on August 5, 1909, and after the first of the year we moved to Flint. My father, Dempster Marshall Howe, had located a house for us near a corner where my Grandfather and Grandmother Spencer lived. The Howe family lived fairly close to us.

Grandfather Samuel Bradish Spencer was a Civil War veteran. He had joined the Union Army when he was 14, by claiming to be the required age of 16, and served as a drummer boy. He was with the 4th Michigan Infantry, Company E. The flag he brought home with him, tattered and torn, is now preserved by the State of Michigan.[1]

---

[1] *The flag Grandfather Spencer carried in the war was on display in the Michigan State Capitol for many years. It was moved in 1989 to the new Michigan State Museum in Lansing. It is preserved there and used in special exhibits, I have been told.*

He had joined the army in 1860, when he was living in Detroit, and was sent to Texas. While there, camping near San Antonio, the regiment with which he was serving was nearly decimated by drinking stagnant water from a lake that had no inlet or outlet. He served during the entire four years of the war between the states. Because he'd been in the service of his country, the government sent him a monthly pension check. It wasn't a large amount and the checks didn't last very long if he could find a store so he could spend it for his needs. He then would plaster houses, shoe horses or mules, and always found ways to earn extra money.

Grandfather Spencer had quite a few law books. He was an avid reader, a serious person who loved writing poetry. He insisted on owning a horse and wagon to supplement his income. He would pick up other persons throw-aways. I would go with him sometimes. Grandma thought I should go with him because he couldn't hear very well. We would get clothes, hats, everything people no longer used. Sometimes Grandma would sort and find things, especially baby clothes, wash them and give them to needy families.

Grandpa chewed tobacco like it was going out of style. When I was with him and the wind was just right, I would get tobacco juice all over me.

Grandmother Mary Jane Willey Spencer owned a hat shop. In this day, everyone wore hats. You would never go to church without a hat. She later accepted secondhand hats and dresses to sell. She and grandpa had adopted a son, Dewey, and were raising him. But her health was deteriorating. She had a breathing problem and the doctor told my Grandfather that it might help her if she lived in California.

Grandfather talked it over with my dad and asked if he would go along on the trip in a covered wagon. Dad said "Yes." So there we were; Grandpa and Grandma Spencer, ten-year-old Dewey, my father, mother, my baby sister Eliza and four-year-old me, all packing up to leave for California. My mother wasn't consulted. Grandfather Spencer and my Dad had two of the strongest wills of any people I've ever known. They made the plans and mother went along.

Actually, mother didn't have much choice. She'd had measles and scarlet fever when a child and had lost most of her hearing. So she was dependent in many ways on those around her. Grandfather Spencer had sent her to the Flint Hearing School where she and grandmother learned sign language. Grandpa had her take piano lessons and she had managed to learn how to play the piano. When she was 20, mother lost the rest of her hearing. But in spite of her handicap, she always found enjoyment in the world around her.

The determination to help grandmother's health improve and the adventurous spirit of my grandfather and father proved to be a blessing. The days to come held many hardships as we made our way westward.

2
TO CALIFORNIA BY COVERED WAGON

With one large black mule, a covered wagon and all the belongings we could pack into it, we were on our way to California in the spring of 1910. Grandfather and Grandmother Spencer with Dewey, who was little more than 10 years old; my father, mother, Eliza and me, all headed out. I took my precious doll along. She had a china head and a soft cloth, stuffed body.

Father and Grandpa Spencer found ingenious ways to make money along the way. They would pick up bottles, wash them and brew what they called "Golden Oil." Then they'd fill the bottles with the oil and keep an eye out for customers. The men would work a few hours or days clearing fields or harvesting crops for farmers. They picked cotton for fifty cents a day when we were in the south.

Daytimes, when the sun was so hot, we would get under the wagon in the shade and wait until it began to get cooler. If it rained, we'd get under the wagon to keep dry. Then we'd wind our way for a few more miles before making camp. We cooked over an open fire, built with old wood we found as we went along. Sometimes we couldn't find much wood to burn, so we would have to go on farther before stopping for the night. We tried to average 20 miles a day, but generally fell several miles below that goal.

The evenings were very cool and the nights were cold. We children slept in the wagon but the adults slept beneath it. To keep the rain and cold wind out, my dad and grandfather would tie a piece of canvas around the wheels of the wagon. Sometimes in the day, if we weren't moving along the trail, they used the canvas for a tent.

I walked behind the wagon as much as I could and it seemed to me that the wagon wheels never stopped. One time though, while we were on a mountain top, a back wheel came off the wagon. My father told us to all look for stones to prop up the axle. There wasn't much room to stand between the wagon and the drop off down the steep side of the mountain, and I was so afraid I began to cry.

"Mamie you can help put grease on the hub of the wheel, and do not look way down anymore," dad said. (He called me Mamie until I was eight years old.) He told me we must have faith that things were going to be all right. He got the wheel on tight enough so it would hold and we could go on down the mountain. With the faith of my father and God, we made it to the next little town of Phoenix in Arizona where we could get the part we needed to repair the wheel.

Grandfather Spencer and dad each had a violin with them. They would play hymns and we all would sing in the evenings around the campfire. My mother's black Bible was read each evening and it was a sacred thing that kept us going in times of stress, I believe. We would ask for guidance through the day and peace at night.

Grandmother Spencer was a staunch church-going lady and swearing was not allowed if she could hear it. But grandpa would start on one of his lengthy bad curses and she would say, "Sam, you will never enter the Kingdom of Heaven that way."

I remember seeing buzzards flying overhead and my dad told me they were eating the carcasses of animals that had died along the trail. Sometimes I could see wild horses off in the distance. Prairie dogs were always around, but never for very long. They would run and hide in their holes.

One day my sister, Eliza, and I were playing near a fence. A terrible wind came up, like a sand storm, and lifted us both up, over the fence and carried us some distance before dropping us down. We were only bruised from the experience, but it frightened us.

I had a different kind of experience on the day my parents discovered I was missing. We were near a village where Indians and Mexicans lived. A couple had taken me to their adobe home, a mud hut, and it was very cool inside. They must have liked me because they made me tortillas which they fried on a bed of coals on the earth floor. They released me a little later and our entire family was glad to have me back safely.

At one time on the trip we saw an Indian funeral going up a steep hill. The Indians all walked along following the corpse which was on a bed of tree limbs. They each dropped a stone as they moved along and they made eerie sounds like moans. But it was their war dances that really upset me, more than anything except thirst.

Sometimes we would settle down for the night and the Indians would start their war dances. They were so close that we could see them as well as hear them.

THE COVERED WAGON WAY

The large mule we had was quite rough. One day my dad and I were leading him to a watering hole and I was walking along near the rear of the mule. He kicked me so hard I was unconscious for a few hours. My mother was very worried about me. I was black and blue later in several places where the mule had kicked me, but fortunately I didn't have any broken bones.

We lived in California for several months, but Grandma Spencer's health did not improve so dad and grandpa decided to go back to Michigan the same way we came, the covered wagon way. By then I was nearly five years old (1911) but the most I recall about this trip was that my Uncle Dewey would catch Horny (Horned) Toads and then make string harnesses for them. He'd attach a harness to a match box to draw behind the toads. Once when we ran out of twine for the harnesses, he felt real bad. He wanted to take some of the toads back to Flint with him and he did take a few, but they died shortly afterward.

3
COOKING ALONG THE TRAIL

Mother and grandmother talked with women who had made the trip out west in covered wagons before we began our journey. They had written down some of the recipes to take with us and use as we went along. Also, when we occasionally met another wagon along the way, the women were happy to visit and almost always spent what little time they could manage in exchanging recipes. Eating was very important along the trail and women spent hours of hard work preparing and cooking food for their families.

We had a cookbook with us, "The Ladies' Aid Society First M.E. Church Cook Book," which had been printed in 1906 in Seattle, Washington. It contained a recipe for Ginger Bread and mother or grandmother made it for very special occasions. No eggs were needed for this recipe, which was a common thing, because fresh eggs were hard to get and hard to keep for very long without refrigeration.

GINGER BREAD

1/2 cup of sugar, 1/2 cup of molasses, 1/4 cup of butter, 1/4 cup of lard, 2 cups flour, 1 tablespoon ginger, 1/2 teaspoon soda. Dissolve soda in 1/2 cup boiling water and add a pinch of salt.

I don't recall any specific directions being given for mixing or baking the Ginger Bread. It was just understood in those days that every woman knew how to bake a cake. And they had to improvise on the trail with reflectors to heat the batter or put it in a Dutch oven until it was done.

We had what we called "Hot Flour Bread," for breakfast quite often. We'd dip slices of bread in hot bacon grease and it tasted very good, especially on cold mornings. There was the delightful smell of bacon frying and, after the men had eaten, we children would dip our bread in the grease. We liked it and it served a double purpose by cleaning the heavy iron fry pans without wasting any of the fat.

Mother was very resourceful about baking bread. We had a barrel of flour on the side of the wagon and she kept a jar of sourdough starter in a safe place inside the wagon. After she'd taken some of the "starter" out of the jar to use for a batch of bread, she'd add a little sugar, water and flour to refill it. Then it would ferment until she needed it again. We were all very careful not to disturb the jar because it was a catastrophe if it ran out. We'd have to borrow a little "starter" and begin the process all over again. We could get a yeast powder, but Mother said it was simply a mixture of cream of tartar and baking soda, and she preferred the sourdough.

Bread was a very important staple in our diets. During the times we were lucky enough to have a milk cow with us, or could find some farmer who would sell us some milk, we often had bread and milk for supper. But making and baking the bread was not easy.

Mother would mix the dough in the morning and let it rise in the bouncing wagon through the day. Then she'd bake it in a Dutch oven placed under hot coals while she cooked supper. How good it smelled around the campfire when she lifted the iron lid. If we were heading out very early in the morning, or if it was raining and we couldn't get a campfire started, we'd eat left-over bread with jam for breakfast.

Mother and grandmother had packed some dried fruit and preserves in our supplies when we left home, but they were soon gone. If we were fortunate enough to find some apples, we'd core and cook them in the big iron kettle over the fire. We'd stir the apples with a long wooden spoon while they simmered. We children didn't mind taking turns stirring, because we'd get to taste the Apple Butter to see if it was getting thick and dark enough to use. We would plan to do this on the days we weren't moving along the trail. It took a long time to make a big batch of Apple Butter. But it didn't last long either. There were six of us on the first trip and 10 of us on the second one, so we ate a lot of food.

When we passed through an area where the corn was ripe, we'd buy some from a farmer. We'd toss the ears into the coals of the campfire and turn them until the husks were black. Then we'd peel off the steaming husks, add some salt and eat the corn right off the cob. Other times, if we made camp early enough, Mother would shave corn off the cob into a bowl and scrape the knife over the bare cob to get all the milky liquid. She'd add a cup of flour, a teaspoon of soda, an egg if she had it, a pinch of salt and just enough milk to make a bubbling batter. She'd drop the batter by a wooden spoonful on a hot iron skillet and we'd have corn dodgers. If we had syrup to go over them, they were especially good. How we loved them.

Stews were fairly frequent for suppers, too. Just about every vegetable we could find would go into the large iron kettle with some water. Sometimes, when the men had been hunting, they'd bring back a rabbit or a squirrel. Mother would brown the meat, add beans, potatoes and any greens she had, and let the stew simmer until it was ready to ladle out into our bowls.

Although we always started out with ample provisions, we had to keep most of the supplies in bags because barrels were heavy and added weight to the wagon. Mother kept some flour in a barrel to be sure it would stay dry. The flour in bags could get wet and we had to watch them very carefully. We had several bags of cornmeal, too. It was used in many ways. We would have cornmeal mush for breakfast, served with milk and brown sugar. If any was left after we'd eaten, it was poured in a bread pan and cooled. Later it could be sliced and fried to a crispy brown.

And there was Johnny cake. It was made by adding a pint of boiling milk to three pints of cornmeal and half a pint of flour. It could be baked on an iron griddle like pancakes, or fried in small flat cakes. It was quicker to make than regular bread and much better if we had some shortening or an egg to beat into the batter. Sometimes a little molasses would give it a different taste. Leftover Johnny cake made another good Sunday evening meal. We'd crumble it into a bowl and pour milk over it.

At times when the day had gone well and we'd make camp early enough, mother would help us make a batch of horehound candy. Although it was primarily used for colds, candy was rare and we enjoyed it whether we had colds or not. She'd bring 6 cups of water to a boil, put 6 cups of loosely packed horehound leaves and stems in the boiling water and let it steep for six minutes. To this brew she'd add 4 cups of sugar, 1-1/4 cups dark cane syrup and 1 tablespoon of butter.

These ingredients would cook in the iron kettle until they reached the hard crack stage. Then we'd skim off any scum and pour it into a 15 x 10 x 1 inch pan and score into pieces before it set. We'd all wait anxiously until it was cool and then have a special treat.

Food supplies were easier to get while we lived in Onaway. I remember one favorite…a vinegar pie…my mother made. The recipe was a standby in lumber camps. This one came from Mrs. Russell Wood of Kalkaska. Viola cooked for her husband's lumber camps in northern Michigan for many years and lumbering was going strong during our stay in Onaway. (The last Wood Brother's Lumber Camp was the Tindle and Jackson Camp at Pellston, about 20 years later.)

VINEGAR PIE

1-1/4 cups sugar, 1-1/2 cups boiling water, 1/3 cup vinegar (natural, not processed), 1/3 cup cornstarch, dash of nutmeg, 3 beaten egg yolks.

Stir the ingredients together and cook until thick and clear. Stir half the mixture into the 3 beaten egg yolks, combine mixture again; place entire filling on the back of a wood range for one minute, add a tablespoon of butter and pour into a baked pie shell. The egg whites could be used to make a meringue topping, but it wasn't necessary because we'd devour the pie in short order. Today you can get almost the same results with a frozen whipped topping.

During World War I, some of the recipes we'd used while camping came in handy. There was an "Eggless, Milkless, Butterless Cake", that we made frequently in Onaway.

Boil together for three minutes:

1 cup water, 2 cups seeded raisins, 1 cup brown sugar, 1/3 cup lard, 1/2 tsp. cinnamon and allspice, 1/2 tsp. salt and 1/8 tsp. nutmeg.

Cool, then sift together: 1 cup flour, 1 tsp. baking powder, 1 tsp. soda. Sift flour mixture gradually into the fruit mixture. Stir until batter is smooth. Bake at 350 degrees until toothpick comes out smooth, about 25-30 minutes if the fire was hot enough in the woodburning stove. These cakes were heavy and we liked them better than the light fluffy cakes that became popular when eggs and butter were available after the war.

The recipes were put back into use during the Great Depression, too, by the cooks who had saved them.

4
OUR SECOND TRIP TO CALIFORNIA

By the time we got back to Flint, we were all tired from the long trip. We'd sold our mules in Indiana and had only one horse left. We'd been able to trade or barter for horses along the trail with Indians who could speak English well enough to talk to us. With others, we'd used sign language to reach agreements. We'd managed until now to keep one or sometimes two fresh horses or mules to get us along the terrible paths and roads.

Dewey started to school again in Flint and life was almost back to normal. (He was my mother's brother and therefore my uncle, but we were so close in age that I always called him "Dewey.") The more my father talked about the beautiful country in California, the more enthusiastic Grandfather Orville Howe became about visiting there. He had a daughter, Etta; and a sister, Frances (called "Frankie") living in Los Angeles, and he was anxious to see them.

Dad was convinced there were more jobs in California and the pay was better than in Michigan, too. They made up their minds to move to California and began making plans. We would go by covered wagon again along part of the Oregon Trail. The two men grew more excited as they plotted the trip and, relying on dad's experience, felt there was little to risk but lots to gain by heading west again. The Gold Rush had long passed, but California was still the land of opportunity.

Within a few months, ten of us started out on the trip. Grandpa Howe, Grandma Cora May Howe and their four youngest children: Margaret (18) Cora Adell (16), Orville Marshall (11), and Earl Nelson (6). In addition there was their eldest son, Dempster, (my dad), along with my mother, Eliza and me, hitting the trail again. I can't recall anyone being unhappy about the prospect. Mother must have been aware of the hard work ahead, but there was a certain amount of freedom, too. She and grandmother could spend time with their families, the regular routine of city life was behind them and living in the fresh air, seeing new sights and meeting new people was an adventure for them as well as for the men.

By now, as a five-year-old, the experiences on the trip were more vivid to me. We would all sing to pass away the time during the day while we were trudging along. And, after a long walk or ride in the wagon, we would stop to build a fire and eat. After we'd eaten, Grandpa Howe and my dad would get out their violins and while they played, we'd sing again around the campfire. The Howe family was very musical. Most of us could sing with harmony, play the piano, organ, violin, or mouth organ.

When there were bad storms, we would sometimes stay in a farmer's barn for the night. Twenty miles or less a day in good weather was considered about the right distance, but the going was slower in the mountains. Sometimes the path had washed out or a large boulder had fallen in our path and we would have to go around it. This didn't leave very much room to pass it on the narrow trail. We would all help the horses go up steep grades, too. The wagon would slip and slide and we would have to work to keep it from falling down hundreds of feet. Then we'd hold on to the wagon to keep it from going too fast down the grades. It was pretty tricky and the roads seemed to be endless.

The mountain canyons were so deep it sometimes seemed miles down to the bottom. We children liked to make echoes in the mountains. We'd shout and the sound would repeat three or four times. We thought it was eerie but fun.

One time on the road to California, we camped on a level spot in the desert but mountains were all round with ledges on them. We saw two Eagles fly back and forth to a nest built in the side of a mountain. We saw one of them carrying what we thought was a small lamb. My dad and grandpa decided to try to get up to the nest for a look. They waited until the Eagles had fed their little ones and dad thought they were through, then he and grandpa started to climb up the mountain. It wasn't easy but they managed to reach the nest and found two baby Eagles in it.

Suddenly, the two parent Eagles returned and swooped down at my dad and grandpa. They nearly lost their footings and were very relieved to get away to safety from the two very strong and angry adult Eagles.

The Black Hills of South Dakota were just as black as they've been described. But they were even blacker to people trying to find a way to California at that time. Wild horses were plentiful and roamed around us. They were plain browns, blacks and some were spotted.

We cleared sage brush and cactus for fifty cents a field for farmers as we went along. Then we used the brush we had scrubbed to build our campfires in the evenings.

Water was a welcome thing when we found any of it. At all old pumps we always left some water in a bucket for priming the pump and hoped the hot sun wouldn't evaporate it before the next person who came along might need it. We rationed our water and it seemed more important than money. Sometimes when we didn't have any water, I would think, "No wonder there are carcasses by the waterholes." The animals had been so thirsty they had drunk the alkaline water that was in some of the waterholes and died. When we came to a stream we bathed, but it didn't happen on a regular basis and none of us children felt deprived.

In Death Valley there were skeletons of animals lying across the desert. It was a sad, dry place for human beings. Once in awhile we'd see flocks of sheep and I wondered where they got their water. Sometimes we would find water at windmills, miles apart, and we could fill our water jugs. Other times we'd think there would be water in a sunken place, where a well had been, but would be disappointed to find it had dried up. This made us worry and wonder where we could find water next.

Grandmother Howe made pancakes often, especially when we were low on supplies. She made syrup to go on them from sugar, water and a few drops of imitation maple flavoring in it. To this day, maple syrup reminds me of the long, hot, dusty, waterless days and the smell of maple makes me feel ill.

Wolves and Coyotes were always around and howling at night. A couple of times our meat or bacon, from wild animals hunted along the way, was all or partially taken if we had not kept the fire going or watched carefully all night. Grandpa and dad carried their rifles most of the time when on foot. Sometimes one would walk and the other would drive the mules or horses. Sometimes they would both walk alongside the horses while grandmother, mother, Margaret, Cora or Orville would hold the reins.

Coming to a city one time, grandma bought some red and black checkered outing flannel to make Earl and me new outfits. She sewed them all by hand and had them completed in no time at all. The only difference between Earl's and mine was that I had a skirt and Earl had short pants. My blouse had cuffs and a little collar.

We were always welcomed and treated well by people along the way. Because my parents and grandparents were ambitious, we had something to eat most of the time. Dad and grandpa were six-footers, so food was necessary for them. We might not have regular times for meals, but we ate at least two times a day…breakfast and a night meal. If we couldn't find a shady place to eat, we would make our own shade with the canvas. When we were low on food we ate more pancakes and imitation maple syrup.

One day we camped not too far from where Indian women could be seen washing their clothes on rocks in a clear stream with a sandy bottom. We washed our clothes right with them. Some Mexican women were there, too. Children were having a good time naked and dancing in the cool water. They dried their clothes on rocks, clean as could be.

Sometimes we would see Indians walking along a road or path. From a distance we could see a few wigwams and children running around and fires burning. The women were dressed in long black skirts with colored tops. They made their clothes from wool they combed from their sheep and grandmother found out that they dyed their colorful tops with juices from plants and bark. They wove their material on looms made from two crude tree limbs. They tied the wool threads around themselves, then put the threads through the strings tied to the looms. They sold their weavings at train stations. The Indian women, and sometimes the men, sat on the ground in the dirt under the depot overhang at the train stations selling baskets, blankets, and jewelry items they'd made.

Dad and Grandpa Howe took turns sleeping so someone would be on guard during the night. But one night grandpa went to sleep and the Indians took our two mules and two horses. They also took my doll which I'd left lying outside the wagon. In the morning my dad and grandpa discovered the animals were missing and were frantic. They started searching and found them in about an hour. But the Indians told them they couldn't have their teams back until we gave them our food and water. So the men bartered with the Indians for things we really needed on the prairie...grain, food and water. They finally let us have our animals but they kept my doll. We gave them what they wanted...and a good talk to grandpa for falling asleep.

After several months on the trail, we finally arrived in Los Angeles.

5
LIVING IN CALIFORNIA

After more than three months in our covered wagon, we were seasoned travelers but our supplies were exhausted. It was good to learn there were job openings in Los Angeles, just as my dad had expected.

Dad and grandpa did carpenter work and Grandma Howe got a job at a large laundry. Many Chinese men worked there and it wasn't long before grandma was supervising the entire laundry.

We lived in the tent while dad and grandpa built a house for us. In the meantime, however, when we left our tent the Gypsies came in and took things. By the time we discovered this was happening, they had already taken grandma's quilt, her watch, a bracelet and some other belongings. From then on, one of us stayed at the tent all the time until we could move into our new house.

Our house was on Redondo Beach, only two blocks away from the Pacific Ocean. It was in the center of a large poppy and carnation field. At night the air was filled with the wonderful smell of the flowers on fresh ocean breezes. We would pick up moonstones and starfish shells along the beach. One day grandma found a large pearl in an oyster. She was offered quite a bit of money for it, so she sold it.

Poinsettias on street corners at Christmas were in large planter boxes. They were beautiful when they were heavy with dew. The cable cars ran close to the ocean. One large store in Los Angeles had part of a floor prepared especially to take care of children while their mothers were shopping. The area was so large that they had outdoor play equipment for children and I thought it was very nice indeed.

When we lived at Riverside, there was a steep hill behind our house and water trickled down into a small stream. My dad made us a wire frame to use and we panned for gold for hours at a time. Sometimes wee particles of gold were found, but not often, and they weren't worth very much.

Occasionally we took a ride in a boat with a glass bottom and it was interesting because you could see the floor of the ocean. Passengers on the boat would throw silver dollars into the water and divers would find them and keep them for their pay. Balloon ascensions were popular in Los Angeles at this time. You could go up in a reed basket under the balloon for about 10 minutes for 50 cents.

While we went to school in Los Angeles, we each had a little garden to tend. It was here that the Colgate company gave each of us a tooth brush and toothpaste to teach us how to clean our teeth properly.

Orange trees were plentiful near our home. Oranges were 15 cents a pail and we could pick them ourselves. In Michigan, oranges had been a big treat and we were lucky to get one at Christmas. We thought this was great when we could eat all we wanted.

Aunt Etta had married a man who owned a hotel and I stayed in her beautiful apartment one night. Aunt Etta and grandpa played evenings in the orchestra pit at the Bijou Theater in Los Angeles. She played the piano and he played his violin. This gave us a little money to help out with so many persons to take care of...ten in all.

If anyone for miles around wanted music in their homes for special occasions, the Howes were always invited because we could sing as well as play the music. We were never without friends and music and places to go. Grandmother and my mother took turns playing the organ at the parties. The violins seemed to know each chord change to go with the organ. Dad and grandpa played all the tunes of the day and all the dance tunes, too.

Grandmother was a beautiful seamstress and could sew almost anything. On Saturdays she would sew for people. Later, we all moved into a larger house with a lot of wood lattice around the porches and grandma took in two men boarders. We had a parrot who had learned some nice words and, from the boarders, some that weren't so nice. So grandmother taught him to say, "Don't say that," and "Good-bye my friend."

A little gold ring on my finger had become so tight that dad said the ring would have to be cut off. I cried as we were getting ready to go one block to the blacksmith's to have it removed. The parrot said, "Good-bye, my friend," and dad promised me another ring. We lived quite a lot with grandpa and grandma. My father was very fond of his mother and as my mother kept losing more of her hearing, he depended on grandmother for making decisions.

Mother sometimes said that my father changed his mind each time the wind blew because he might have told her one thing and then, after discussion with grandmother, he thought another way. But despite the fact that by now she'd lost almost all her hearing, mother managed to take care of the world around her. I thought that with Grandmother Howe's courage and my father's strength, we could do anything.

The Bible was kept in mind, read regularly, and talked about in some heated discussions. Attending church was expected and kept our lives constant with the musical talents we all had.

One day we went aboard a large ship docked on the ocean where the public was allowed. We saw what we thought were Hindus dressed in their native dress, mashing grapes with their bare feet in a large iron kettle. Three men were singing and making wine. I enjoyed the smell of the salty breezes on the waterfront.

We visited "Old Baldy" sometimes on Sundays after church or we rode the cable car along the ocean. But we spent many hours at the park on Redondo Beach. The band shell was there and wooden chairs were lined up for the public to sit on, so they could hear the music and enjoy the refreshing breezes from the ocean. People came from all over to hear the band on weekends.

The Fourth of July at Redondo Beach was quite an occasion. I had been given a small package of firecrackers and was lighting one when they all caught fire. Before I knew it, my hand was badly burned. The pain left a little when someone gave me an ice cream cone.

Grandpa Howe bought 25 honeybee hives and we sold honey in Redondo Beach. He showed me how to help him collect the honey and the bees never seemed to bother either of us.

We all enjoyed living in California for about a year. There was almost always sunshine, birds singing and lush green flower plants growing with beautiful blossoms. But Grandmother and Grandfather Howe had left five daughters behind and they decided to go back to Michigan. So once again we began to pack our things, stock up supplies and say, "Good-bye," to the friends we'd made.

6

HEADING BACK TO MICHIGAN

It wasn't an especially happy day when we headed out in our covered wagon for the return trip to Michigan. This was the fourth trip, either to or from California, within the past three years. By now we were fairly familiar with the routes and aware of many problems we might encounter. We tried to make preparations for any emergencies. Still, we packed too many things in the wagon for it to carry and were sorry about it later.

Although Earl was only four months older than I was, he was the youngest child in my father's family and was my uncle. I never called him "Uncle Earl," though, and it may have been because he was the baby in their family and I was the eldest child in our family. In any event, he seldom found much to like about our travels and never liked to talk about the trips when he grew up. The rest of us children didn't mind. As long as we were with our families we felt everything would work out fine. But it must have taken a lot of courage for my mother to face another 2,000 mile trek across the mountains and plains. She was going to have a third child and she wasn't feeling well.

We had smelling salts for mother when she became faint and she had to use them often. She did a lot of walking beside or behind the wagon, but she could get in the wagon anytime she felt like it. Of course, bumping along in the wagon couldn't have made her feel much better.

Going back on this trip were Grandfather and Grandmother Howe and their children: Dempster (my father), Margaret, Cora, Orville, and Earl; my mother, Eliza and me. Etta remained in California with her new husband.

There were many hills and mountains to cross and the horses got some relief going down them. But going up the steep slopes was another thing...they tired easily. We had our white bulldog "Mastiff" along with us and he made a good watchdog.

By the time we'd camped a few nights and reached the desert, it became apparent that our water was nearly gone and there was none to count on ahead. There was quite a discussion then, but it was decided Mastiff would have to be put out of the way or sold. Then, to save the horses energy, we must unload every article we could get along without. So we piled some of our belongings all together and left them behind. As we continued along the trail through the desert, we dropped even more things by the way.

We realized the horses we had could not compare to mules when it came to hauling the wagon. So the horses were traded for two mules and a donkey for one of us to ride on when we became weary of walking. Later on, we crossed a small bridge with the wagon, but the donkey refused to budge. We tried for one or two hours to get him across. Finally, an Indian came along and he saw our predicament. He led the donkey across the bridge without any trouble. That incident cost us 25 cents, which my dad paid him.

THE COVERED WAGON WAY

The campfire was always kept burning at night unless one of the men fell asleep. Grandpa Howe was usually the guilty one. One night, when he'd gone to sleep, the fire went out. I woke up screaming and Aunt Margaret did too. I slept on one side of the wagon, she slept in the center and Earl was on the other side. A mountain lion had reached up and over me and Margaret to Earl. I could feel his claw and fur over my arm. He was scared away somehow, probably by our screams. Dad shot at him, but he ambled away. I never forgot that soft touch from the mountain lion.

We halted our trip and lived in a house in Phoenix, Arizona, for a couple of months and went to the doctor there. I believe it was because my mother was having a hard time with her pregnancy. Grandmother Howe began teaching at an Indian Mission because the regular teacher was ill. Earl, Orville and I went to school there, but not for long because their regular teacher returned.

There was an Indian making jewelry right next to our house and I spent many hours watching him turn out lovely articles of silver jewelry. I could go watch him if Earl or Orville was with me.

Aunt Margaret, a pretty 20-year-old, and the young doctor became friends. He wanted her to stay and marry him, but she decided to go on with us and so he gave her an all-white donkey to take with her.

Now we had two mules and two donkeys to feed and water, which was a problem. Especially the water. We had a small barrel on the side of the wagon and we would fill leather sacks with water from it for the animals to drink.

One night while we were asleep, the barrel sprung a leak and we had no water in the morning. It caused my parents and grandparents a lot a worry, but a day later we found a small stream. They fixed the barrel and, after we tasted the water, they filled the barrel with it and we used it. We knew it would be good to drink because there were no buzzards around like there were near alkaline watering holes where animals had died.

While we were still in Arizona, my dad and grandfather ran over an 8-foot rattlesnake. They cured the skin themselves so they could bring it back and show people in Michigan how large the snakes were out there. I don't know if it was the same snake or not, but a rattler did bite Earl and Grandfather Howe took him to an Indian medicine man and Earl survived.

We would always go to church on Sunday, when we were near one, no matter what denomination it was. Once I had a little verse to say at church. It went like this:
> "The crumbs that fall upon the floor,
> The crumbs I cannot eat,
> There's so many little hungry ones
> Would think it quite a treat."

By the time we were 300 miles from home, mother became very ill and dad decided she should take the train back to Michigan. Eliza and I went with her and were entranced by two lion cubs a lady had with her in the car we were on. When we finally reached Flint, we were in all the papers again.

Soon after we'd returned to Michigan my brother Marshall Bradish was born in Pontiac on March 8, 1912. Dad had found a job near there with an automobile company.

7
LIFE IN ONAWAY

Having been so independent for several years, it must have been difficult for my father to find himself back in Michigan with a regular job in an automobile factory. He had a son now, too, and he must have considered what the future would hold for our family if we stayed where we were. Grandfather and Grandmother Spencer had moved with Dewey to the village of Onaway, where Grandfather had bought a "Five and Dime" store and gone into business.

The Lobdell Wood Rim Company was located in the village and my father wrote to inquire about working for them. Onaway was more than 100 miles to the north of Flint, in Presque Isle County, but I guess after the thousands of miles we'd covered in the long trips to and from California, the distance didn't seem very far to him now.

Lobdell's Wood Rim factory made wood rims and spokes for automobiles. They replied with a promise of a foreman's job for my father and said they had a house we could move into. So in 1913 we made the trip north, moving everything we had again. Grandfather and Grandmother Howe, Orville and Earl moved along, too.

When we arrived in Onaway we found that the house we'd been promised was still occupied. So until the family moved out, we had to live in a log cabin the company had in their camp 14, about five miles from Onaway. In addition to the log cabin, there was a large barn on the property and this was where the company kept a herd of steers. For our rent, we could feed and take care of the livestock. We'd take them to a nearby stream for water once a day and at night we'd bring them in from the fields and put them in the barn.

One day each month we would go to town and get groceries. When we got there, I'd walk behind my mother and grandmother because they used sign language and I was embarrassed. By now mother's hearing was almost totally gone.

During the several months we lived in the cabin, I learned a lot about nature, cattle and trout fishing.

The schoolhouse was more than a mile-and-a-half away. One day when Orville, Earl and I were walking home from school it was snowing just awful. Earl and I decided we would sit in a hollow tree stump and rest. Orville, being oldest, kept on walking. By the time he got home, it was getting late so my folks started out to find Earl and me. They finally located us, covered with snow and sound asleep in the hollow stump. When we got back, grandmother warmed us up with blankets in front of the woodburning cookstove and gave us whiskey slings. We could have frozen if we'd had to stay there all night. But they had found us in time and we were all right.

Sometimes after school I'd go with Orville and Earl to round up the livestock and put them in the barn for the night. We had to cross a trout steam near the cabin and it was full of trout. The trout splashed noisily as they were swimming against the flow of the stream and, fortunately, the horses we rode or drove were not frightened by them.

I became close friends of two of the girls at school. One family had quite a few cows and made butter and buttermilk to sell. They would ask me over for a weekend and I enjoyed that family very much.

When we finally moved into our long awaited house in Onaway, I had another family of friends. They had a piano and the two girls could sing and were about my age, nine years old. We would sing harmony for hours at a time and enjoy each others company. Their names were Armanta and Gardeline Blair. In later years the Blairs had a large trailer company in Alma. Sometimes the school principal's son, Keith Odell, would sing with us. I liked him very much. I also stayed at the house of a friend who was adopted. It was just a little way outside Onaway and by the cemetery. The family took care of the cemetery.

There were many things for us to do and we were busy all the time doing one thing or another. When raspberries were in season we picked pails of them while always keeping an eye out for black bears which were often nearby. We took a train ride to Mullett Lake for the July 12th, Orangeman's Lodge picnic. The charge was 25 cents for the train from Onaway to Mullett. One time there was a race to run by the train depot and I won 50 cents.

Other memories I have are when I was in the fifth grade. I was chosen to be in the class play but I couldn't be in it without a certain dress. I cried until Grandmother Howe found the material and made the dress for me. There was the time the congregation of the church was asked to go to the minister's potato patch and pick potato bugs from the leaves before they were sprayed with Paris green. (A preparation containing arsenic, used as an insecticide). And one day my dad took my sister Eliza and me to the store to buy Eliza a pair of slippers. I put up such a fuss he had to buy me a pair, too.

We had a promotion in town to sell Cloverine salve. I worked very hard to get the top prize...a pony...but I ended up with a gold locket instead. Some of my time I would pick up bottles, clean them and sell them to the drug store for three cents each.

There was that most important event when we gathered at the train station for the arrival of my mother's new piano. Then every youngster in town ended up walking along beside it, as it was delivered to our house.

One day I stopped in to Grandfather Spencer's store and asked him if I could have a couple of cookies. He asked me if I had any money to pay for them and I said, "No." He said he was sorry, but he couldn't give them to me without any money. So I sat on the steps until the store closed and he finally gave in and gave me the cookies. Then I went home. It could be that I'd inherited some of that "strong will" from my grandfather.

Grandmother Spencer would take me to her friends to sing for them. For one sick friend, I sang the song, "Jesus wants me for a sunbeam, to shine on him each day." Everyone said I had a good voice and I enjoyed going on these visits. They generally had some cookies and milk for me, too.

We could only buy our groceries in two places, Gumm's store and the Company store. The family across from Gumm's store was a Jewish family by the name of Friedman and they owned the shoe repair shop next to their home. I would start fires for them in their stoves on Saturdays, because their religion prohibited them from doing this chore. I noticed, though, it didn't stop them from building stove fires on Saturdays in their shoe repair shop. I also did their dishes on Saturdays. This earned me 25 cents. One day I washed all of their dishes in the same water and they threw them out. I felt terrible. I didn't understand their religious order. Their daughter, Mina Friedman, was one of my best friends.

The "Company Store" was a meeting place on Saturday nights and holidays. The store was for families who worked at the factory and used their credit to buy food and other items. The cost of what they bought was taken out of their paychecks. Square dances were held on the floor above the store and sometimes everyone would bring things to eat. Other times there would be box socials, put on by the factory, and there would be dancing then, too. My parents would play the organ and violin. Then grandpa and grandma would take turns. When it came time to go home, in the winter, I'd be pulled on the large toboggan my dad had made from left over wood at the Lobdell factory. We children did a lot of sliding in the winters on Tower Hill and Galt Hill, too.

We were allowed to have the scrap wood thrown away at the factory and my dad and grandpa made other things from the wood, too. Dad made fishing lures and plaques. He painted scenes on the plaques and sold them or gave them as prizes to the children who won races. The discarded wooden wheel rims were salvaged for us children to play with. We learned to roll the hoops so they would come back to us. We had contests with our young friends and a slight knoll in front of our house became a feature in the competition. We could see Black Lake, five miles away from our house, and years later (1964) Onaway High School was built on the property.

Despite the fact that father had a regular job and we had a nice home to live in, the years in Onaway were not easy. Mother gave birth to Phillip Abraham on April 4, 1915. World War I was declared on April 6, 1917 and as time passed, supplies such as sugar and coffee were scarce. Several of the young men had to leave for the service.

Mother had another baby, Dorothy Marjorie, born on February 27, 1918, and less than four months later, Eliza died. She had become ill and we called the doctor, but she died two days later from what was diagnosed as acute gastro-infection. Eliza was only nine years and nine months old when she died on June 2, 1918. These were sad days. World War I was still going on and there was much sickness from influenza. Everyone stayed home as much as possible so they wouldn't catch the flu from other people. Stores were closed and even church services weren't held, except for funerals.

But November 11, 1918 was a joyous day when the war ended. The town went wild when word came that peace had been declared. People danced in the streets and had great faith that everything would soon be back to normal. Grandfather and Grandmother Spencer left soon after to return to Owosso. And when Lobdells Wood Rim Company burned down in 1919, we left Onaway, too. Grandfather and Grandmother Howe, Orville and Earl; my mother and father, me, Marshall, Phillip and baby Dorothy Marjorie all left by train and joined the others in Owosso.

I was 13 years old and we'd lived in Onaway for six years, the longest we'd lived in one place. It was hard to leave, but once again adventure called. I liked riding on the train much better than bumping along the covered wagon way.

8
ON TO OWOSSO AND LANSING

In 1919 we left Onaway and moved to Owosso, a short distance from Corunna where I'd been born. My parents had lived in Corunna for about five years before we'd moved to Flint. From there we'd made the first and second trips to California the covered wagon way, returned to Flint and then moved to Onaway. So now we'd come almost a full geographic circle.

Traveling wasn't easy in those days but we were certainly mobile, as they say today. The chief difference was, I think, that we moved from place to place as complete generational families. So the changes in our locations were not disruptive to us children. We were a stable family. Dad was the eldest son in his family and was close to his mother, my Grandmother Howe. Mother was close to her parents, my Grandmother and Grandfather Spencer, because she was their only daughter.

The Corunna, Bancroft, Owosso area was our last stop. Grandfather Orville M. and Grandmother Cora Howe had their own home with young Orville and Earl. Grandpa Howe's sister, Etta, came to Owosso, later. Grandfather and Grandmother Spencer had their own home with Dewey. Grandma Spencer had two brothers, Minor C. Willey and Elliott A. Willey, who also lived in Owosso. In our family home we had mother, father, Marshall, Phillip, Dorothy and me. Donald was born on

November 7, 1919, soon after we'd moved to Owosso. Several years later my mother had twin boys who weighed 8-1/4 and 8 pounds, but they were stillborn.

Dewey married Florence G. Safferd a year after we'd moved to Owosso. They were married in Flint, on March 29, 1920, and he had a job as a buffer in a stove company. They had five children, all boys: Dewey, Daniel, Jack, Milo and Lyle. They lived in Owosso, although Jack was in Arkansas in later years and was killed in World War II.

My father had a job as foreman in the American Malleables, a sand casting factory where they made parts for automobiles. I went to Wadsworth School and sometimes after class I would go down to the factory and make cores of sand so hot iron could be poured over them.

Life was fun in Owosso. Because I was the eldest child in the family, more was expected of me in some respects. On the other hand, I wasn't held back by any precedents and could go my own way...within limits. It wasn't long before I'd become acquainted with other teenagers. All the neighbors and friends would get together and sit under a large Maple tree at "Pittsburg Corners," where a church was located. On the other corner was a country store. This was at the intersection of Grand River Road and M-52.

It was at one of these gatherings, under the lovely old Maple tree, that I met John Morrison Beardslee. John and I were married on December 13, 1923, when I was 17. We lived in Owosso the first year we were married and our daughter, Lillian, was born there in 1924.

Then John was offered a job through his cousin, as a tool maker in the Reo Company in Lansing. We moved to Lansing early in 1925 and after we were settled in, I joined the Potter Park Methodist Church. We had two more daughters. Beverly Ann was born on December 23, 1929 and Joyce Kathryn was born on September 13, 1931.

While the girls were young I did quite a bit of singing, with the lead in the plays sponsored by the Monday Night Volley Ball Club. I was also a judge for the Olds Talent Show each year for five years. When the girls were in school, and Lillian was in college, I started working for the Cedar Street Recreation Center and was supervisor of after school activities for children in the neighborhood schools. I taught weaving, metal enameling, ceramics and many other crafts. I was there for 26 years. During this time I also belonged to the Women's Society of the Methodist Church and continued my membership for 50 years.

We moved to East Lansing in April, 1947, where we had a new home built. I then attended the Asbury Methodist Church until 1988. We bought the lot south of our house and this became John's garden which he dearly enjoyed later in life. He provided vegetables for the neighbors and us and the children, too. We had been married almost 65 years when John had a stroke and fell, breaking his sternum. He developed complications and died at the St. Lawrence Dimondale Center on May 22, 1988. He was buried in the Chapel Hill Memorial Gardens, in Lansing.

Meanwhile, Lillian studied for two years at Michigan State University and taught in the Dewitt Elementary School. (Later, she continued her studies until she had her Master of Arts degree in education from Wayne State University.) Beverly obtained her license as a social worker and was employed by the State of Michigan. Joyce, after a year at Michigan State University, married Charles Reason and moved to Fowlerville.

After John died, I moved to Fowlerville in December 1988. I lived there by myself until May of 1990. By then I'd given up driving and decided to return to Lansing. I moved into the Delta Retirement Home where there are many activities as well as my life-long interest in arts and crafts to enjoy. I've done some oil paintings and even sold a few. Making Santa Clauses in ceramics for my grandchildren and great-grandchildren is another project I've undertaken.

In March 1996, my daughters held a surprise 90th birthday party for me in Beverly and Wayne Jackson's home in Lansing. Beverly sent letters to about 150 of my friends and relatives suggesting they send me birthday cards. "We can't think of any gift Mother would enjoy more than hearing from you," she wrote.

Thirty people arrived at Beverly's home to help celebrate with a dinner and a three tiered cake. They enjoyed looking over all my cards, nearly as much as I had enjoyed receiving them.

May at about 4 years old with the muff Aunt Margaret gave to her.

About 1909. May with her parents and sister.
From left to right: Dempster, May, Eliza, Estella.

*1916.
May, 10,
with her bunny
and Grandpa Spencer.
Saginaw, Michigan.*

*1925.
Grandma and Grandpa Howe.
Owosso, Michigan.*

*1922.
"My Sis and Me."
May, 16, with her
sister Dorothy, 4.*

1921. May, 16.

1926. The Howe Family. Owosso, Michigan.
Clockwise from left: Phillip A. Howe, Dorothy M. (Howe) Ordway,
May C. (Howe) Beardslee, Marshall B. Howe, Dempster M. Howe,
Donald R. Howe, Estella M. (Spencer) Howe.

1926. May's parents, Estella and Dempster Howe, in their Salvation Army uniforms.

1955. Estella and Dempster Howe on their 50th Wedding Anniversary.

Samuel B. Spencer, May's maternal grandfather, was the last surviving Civil War veteran in Shiawassee County when he died in 1939. He enlisted in Lincoln's army in 1863 when he was only fourteen years old and served for the duration of the war.

1938. "My Three Girls."
May and John's children pose at a family reunion in Bentley Park, Owosso, Michigan. From left: Lillian, Beverly, Joyce.

1973. May and John on their 50th Wedding Anniversary.

1996. May Beardslee Howe.

1995. "Some of My Oil Paintings."
May continues to pursue her love of painting and ceramics for her own enjoyment as well as that of her patrons.

1996. "My Great Grandchildren."
Top row: Jessica Bogle; Bottom row from left: Jennifer Stanley,
David Stanley, May (Howe) Beardslee, John Stanley, Joshua Bogle.
(Not pictured: Richard Cochran and Katie Campbell)

1996. "My Lansing Family."
(From left) Top row: Michael Stanley, Mary Bogle, Raymond Bogle,
Emiley Brown; middle row: Katherine Stanley, Wayne Jackson,
Beverly Jackson, Donna Mathews, Richard Stanley, Joshua Bogle;
bottom row: Jennifer Stanley, David Stanley, May (Howe)
Beardslee, John Stanley, Jessica Bogle.

This family tree traces May's roots back to her great-great-great-grandparents who first wed in England and then traveled to America on the Mayflower.

Lillian May   Beverly Ann   Joyce Kathryn
└─────────────────┬─────────────────┘
May Castella Howe ══ John Morrison Beardsley
            │
Dempster M. Howe ══ Estella Spencer
                              │
                    Samuel B. Spencer ══ Mary Willey

Orville M. Howe ══ Cora Goodnow

Marshall Howe ══ Caroline McLain

Albert Orville Howe ══ Orilla Fuller

Parley Howe ══ Betsy Root

For a complete family history, including all brothers, sisters, and offspring, please refer to the chapters on the Howe family and the Spencer family in the Appendix.

APPENDIX

FRANKIE HOWE'S LETTERS AND RECOLLECTIONS

LETTERS WRITTEN BY FRANCES (FRANKIE) HOWE FULLER. (The original spelling, punctuation and grammar have been retained.)

Sparta, Michigan May 14, 1923

Dear Sister and Brother and All
      Cora and Orville

Well dear ones I don't know as you can read my writing- I know as you said once there is no use of complaining- but we have had a hospital here about ever since Xmas- both Charlie and myself still under the Dr. care- had the Gripp the first of our sickness- begin to get a little better so I could get up from bed then Chas was taken more sick in bed and had to get a neighbor to do the chores. Then I took a relapse, in bed again.

Then Chas got so he could get outdoors to do his own chores - but not long- then he was taken down the 3rd time and then he had newmonia - he was in bed for near 2 weeks and then we had to hire a man to do the chores and had to hire another neighbor to plough and put the oats in for it was geting late for oats - he had abcesses in his head and throat when these abcesses broke it caused spasms of larynix of the throat. Then here I got something similar to his throat disease and here we are both not able to do much but we are looking to be better someday.

I would have written you before but I could not stand it. I have just got off the bed this p.m. for I hafto lie down often, but I want to tell you and all the rest-Orville-Earl-Dempster-his wife. I am so glad you have joined God's Army have stepped out of darkness into light - I hope and Pray you will always walk in the light and not faint by the road side. Oh Cora and Orville and all the others be steadfast. Cling close to God ask of him in prayer and he will hear you. God Be Praised Forever More.

May 15 - had to give up writing till this 2 p.m. Now Cora as to your questions I will ans all I know of them and I can tell all for mother and Henry both had all these down- on the MClain side and most all on the Howe side and Aunt Ann Unger told me more about our ancestors on the Howe side when she was to see us in 1917 - six years ago.

1 Question- there were no marriage license given as long ago as when mother and father were married. Nor was there any marriage license even when you and Orville were married or Chas and myself but got a Marriage Certificate from whom married the couples - untill later in years the government passed a law to compel the County to issue license - this came in law after we- Chas and I were married - but of course had to show the license to whom marries the couple before the minister or Justice, which ever done the job-

---

You know Mother Howe couldn't get her Pension for 2 years after Father died for the reason she couldn't produce her Marriage Certificate - for when they moved here from York state they lost their certificate in some way - but after 2 years had passed after Father died (while in the Union army) some lawyer in Flint took it in hand and wrote to York state for an affadavit from witnesses who attended Father and mothers wedding - and the Lawyer got the witnesses all right so she, Mother, then got her Pension. So no one knows as to where her Certificate went to-

Father Howe was born May 7, 1828- he was 23 years old when married in 1852 and died on Dec 15- in 1862- Mother told me dozen of times she and Father lived together just 10 years and here the figures are: married in 1852 and died in 1862. Suspect then he was 33 years old when he died- he died in Louisville- Kentucky and was buried there- Dec. 1862 on the 15th day of the month at 8 oclock a.m.

And now Mother was born in 1824, was 4 years older than Father, lacking about 12 days- they were married the last day of Oct 1852 and she was 27 years old on the 12 of Nov 1852 so you see for your self- Mother Howe was 80 yrs, 3 months & 8 days when she died. You see her birthday was the 12 of Nov. 1904 and died in March 1905, which makes her age as I have told you above, 3 months and 8 days old over 80 years old.

   Mother Howes maiden name was Caroline Perlina Mclain and her mothers name was Lorania Borough and this Grandmother- Mothers name was like M.urrell a French lady by birth. All the other relation of our Mother Howe is Pure Blooded Scotch the Hiland scotch only a little French blood remains in ours.

<u>Second beginning</u> here Cora you see this Loraina Burough married Grand Father Mclain he was Mother Howes Father his Father or Great Great Grand Father came here direct from Scotland with his scotch Bride - only this Loraina Burough who married Grandfather McLain- it was her Grandmother that was the French Lady - Mother used to tell me she remembered this French Grandmother of hers. She said she was a small woman but very pretty. Mother was only six years old when her mother died. Mother said this great-grandmother married a Scotch man

so all of her ancesters were Scotch but this one Great-Grandmother.

Now Father Howe's Fathers name was Albert Orville Howe, he married a young English girl for his wife, her name was Orrilla Fuller - this Grandfather Howe of ...children- his Fathers name was Parley Howe - he married a young lady by the name of Betsy Root. All this strain of our Father Howes are strictly English- this Great Grand Father married Betsy Root in England and came over here to America on the Mayflower.

Aunt Ann Unger told me all about the Howes ancestors as far back as she knew, and the others she didn't know about were left over in England=

So Cora and Orville-Henry our Brother was name Henry Albert, Albert after his Grand Father and Brother Orville was named Albert and the second Boy took the last name of his GrandFather Howe, his father (I mean Orville's Father) named him Orville Benjiman Howe, Benjiman was fathers name, Marshall Benjiman Howe...as far as we know of the Howes and then marriages comes as I can draw it out on the other side and you can see it better.

Parley Howe-married to Betsey Root in England and came direct to York state on the Mayflower.
Albert Orville Howe married Orrilla Fuller here in New York state
Our father Marshall Benjiman Howe married our mother
Caroline Perlina Mclain in York state in 1852
so you see here is our father and mother, our Grand Father and Grand Mother - then our Great-Grandfather and (Great)-Grandmother - all Howes.

Now here are Mother and Fathers ages when born- when married- and when died.

Mother Howe was born on Nov 12-1824
Father Howe was born on May 7-1828
They were married the 31 of Oct 1852
Father died on the 15 of Dec-1862
They lived together 10 years before Father died 1862
           Married 1852
Mother Howe died on the 20 of March 1905
  she was 80 years old on the 12 of Nov. 1904, so you see she lived from the 12 of Nov till the 20 of March..over in the new year of 1905
  80 years 3 months and 8 days old

Now ... Cora and Orville, I want you to listen here to what I am telling you for it stands for the right of our parents who are gone above and we hope to meet them again some beautiful day.
This is what my dear Mother has told me more than once and told me to remember so I could tell you all if you didn't know.

Mother and Father were married- Father 23 when married and our Mother 27- you see mother was 4 years older than Father and they lived together 10 years so Father was 33 years old when he died—and in their 10 years of married life they had 5 children- now listen- married in 1852.
  Henry was born on Jan 13 -1854
  Frances E. was born on Aug 3rd-1856
  Orville was born on the 26 of Dec - 1858
  A little brother was born on the 26 of March - 1860
    he died at birth and was buried west of Clio-
  Carrie was born on the 3rd of Sept - 1862

You see by these figures just how old we children are- Just take each of our birth years and subtract same from this 1923 the year of our Lord.
    ———————————— continued to 3rd

the 3rd leaf

We children 3 of us   Henry- myself (Frankie) and Orville were born in New York state the little bro that died at birth and Carrie were born in Mich ...

Father came home from Saginaw where the Soldiers had gone to drill and recruit— he got a leaf or a Furlow as he called it - for 3 days before his Regiment had to go South he came home on the 7 oclock train P.M. from Saginaw on the 2nd day of Sept 1862 - and on the 3rd of Sept the next morning after he got home Carrie was born- he staid till the 7 of Sept at home then went back to Saginaw to join his Regiment and in 2 weeks from then our Father left with the other soldiers for the South never to return- he died the same year he went there in- he went in Sept 1862 and died on the 15 of Dec 1862- Orvilles birth day was on the 26 of that same Dec in 1862- he was 4 years old in just 11 days after his Father died- I was 6 years old in Aug on the 3rd and Henry was 8 years old- the little Brother would have been 2-   Carrie about 3 months old when he died and she will be 61 years old this next birth day 3rd of Sept. I will be 67 years old on the 3rd of Aug if I live out this year- Orville will be 65 years old his next birthday- the little brother that died at birth would have been 63 - he was born when Orville was 2 years old-   Orville was a baby in his Mothers arms when we moved from York state here

and now Henry- if he had lived- he would have been 70 years old his next birthday in Jan 1924- but just in this year of 1923 he would be called 69 yers old- You take the years we were all born in and substract them from this present time of 1923 and see-

Mother did have a memory book of all our own ages but it got burnt up when the old home in Pine Run burnt- but she knew it all and told Carrie and me of it many a time and I set it down or I couldn't have remembered so well, you see there is two years apart in all of us children ages- in ten years of their married life Father and Mother had 5 children

Well Cora this is May 18 - I had to stop writing for I got so nervous I couldn't write at all. Just the night of the 16- I was up with Charlie at 2 a.m. putting hot cloths wrung out of water and turpentine, a tablespoon of turpentine to a pt of water and just as hot as I could stand to wring the woolen cloth out of this, to keep him from choking to death- it is Ulcers or little abcesses that form in the throat and this hot preparation applied to the throat penetrates to the ulcers and then they break and come up- Oh its just awful to see him suffer when he has these spells- the Dr. says it is the genuine Flue - he is better this morning. Glen's wifes Father is dying of the same thing Charlie is having- I presume he is dead by this morning- he lives at Linden, Genesee Co., just 4 miles south of Flint- his name is Rev George K Fairbanks- if you look in your paper you will probably see his death- Lulu Glens wife went yesterday to Linden and 2 brothers - one lives in Kansas- the other in New York City- was telegraphed for brothers of Lulus I mean he- Mr Fairbanks was a Methodist Minister- Glen came over to see to us last night and tell us about it- he will go if he (Fairbanks) dies but the Dr said he was past living when they telegraphed for the children- see he is Glens father in law—

Well Cora I have missed one of your questions Old Dr. Hooper doctored Mother and I presume he would be the one to issue the death Certificate. Of course I don't know for Mother died over to Carries home but I never heard anything about it. Maybe Carrie and George knows.- well I am sending a snapshot of one of the pictures of the Howe in Mich. Orville and myself were born in New York - Henry was here in 1909 and took pictures of diferent places- I have one left of the same house only another view - and I am sending it to you Orville so you can see the house you were born in.

Now Cora dear sister- if I haven't answered all your questions don't be afraid to tell me and if I can I will ans all you ask if I know- this is a long letter and maybe you can't read it- I am in such a nervous shake I can't hardly write any more- I hope you and Orville will like this little picture of his old birth place in Baldwinville, New York state, Cayuga Co. The plant in front of the house is tobacco plants growing. Henry said this same piece of land was in tobacco when father sold it - 1859 - and came here to Mich- When you was only a year old- he says he could remember it well, of course he was the oldest of us all but (not?) very old at the (time)

I have to go and lie down again so hope this letter will be pleasing to you both- if you had a little frame with a glass over the picture then it would keep it from fading. Good by till I hear from you- write me soon as you can if Charlie or I get worse- I mean seriously worse- we will let you know   someway

Lovingly your Sister, Frankie ... Fuller Give my best wishes to all

Ps do you know Glen Decker came back to Flint last winter- well he did- he his wife and children and they are there now some where

Sparta, Michigan June 18, 1923

Dear Sister and Bro. and nephew
   Cora and Orville,

I rec'd your very dear and welcome letter a while ago - was glad to hear you were all well....
Well Cora and Orville- dear sister and bro - You ask if I wasn't mistaken about our Mothers Blood in the Scotch. No No- I am all right as to her ancestors blood - her people the Mclains were what is called the Highland Scotch and then there is the Lowland Scotch. The Highland Scotch come from the Northern part of Scotland and the Lowland Scotch come from the southern part of Scotland.

When Brother Henry was here to see me the last time he told me he had been looking up the Scotch Blood in our veins and also he had traced the English on our Fathers side and he found true Blood on both sides. Our Father was a true English man. Our Mother came from the Highland Scotch only except this one great grand mother Murrell- but the great grand father Murrell was a Highland Scotch- same as all of mothers name- the Mclains. I think her grandmother Murrell's name was Betsy Parnell. She was the French girl that Grand Father Murrell - he a scotch man - married. This Great-Grandfather Murrell's Mothers name was McLain and she married this Murrell and Murrell's son married the French girl. (Frankie spelled Murrell with one "r" at times.)

Well you can see I have run out of paper. Will hafto finish on this kind not so good either. So as Henry found our parents ancestors as our Mother had told me. You see Henry looked up the Mclains the Scotch to know about this big heir ship. Property that so much as been said about. Henry didn't leave one board unturned over, he went from the bottom of it - up to the last Survivor- It was our Great Grand Father Mclain -our mother's own Grandfather Mclain who owned all this enormous property. Now his name was Uriah Mclain, the Father of our own Grand Father, Mothers father, his name was Vansensler Mclain. Then Great GrandFather Mclain was born in Scotland a Highland Scot as they call them.

Married there in Scotland to a girl by the name of Elizabeth Davenport and came here to America when it ws a wilderness 250 years ago and it was him who took up the land from the Government - then one of his sons by the name of Abner Mclain, a brother to our grandfather Mclain, that signed papers to some land agts for all this estate for a small sum of only fifty dollars to save himself from prison. In those days the county could imprison a young man for a small debt and old Uncle Philander Mclain, who used to live in Swartz Creek, signed the papers with this bro. of his to save his bro- but they are both dead now - I don't know how it will come out - Well, I must close, Chas or myself is very poorly. Write when you can. Love and best wishes to all.

Your sister Frankie E. Fuller

Note inserted above:
No Cora there is no dutch blood in our mothers veins.

Note on side of paper:
Do you know Carrie- Geo- Goldie his Mom are on the road back to Mich

HOWE FAMILY

PARLEY HOWE married **BETSY ROOT** in England and came direct to York State on the Mayflower. They had a son, Albert Orville Howe. (Author's great-great-great-grandfather)

ALBERT ORVILLE HOWE married Orrilla Fuller in York State and they had a son, Marshall Benjamin Howe. (Author's great-great-grandfather)

MARSHALL BENJAMIN HOWE (Author's great-grandfather) was born May 17, 1828. He married Caroline McLain on October 31, 1852. He sold land in Baldwinville, New York in 1859 and moved his wife and their three children to Michigan. They had another son, born on March 26, 1860, who died at birth. Marshall joined the Union Army in Saginaw in 1862, where he was in training. He came home on a furlough on September 2, 1862. The next morning, September 3, their fourth child "Carrie" was born. Marshall stayed at home until September 7, before returning to his Regiment in Saginaw. Two weeks from then, he left with the other soldiers for the south never to return. He died on December 15, 1862, at the age of 33, in Louisville, Kentucky, and was buried there.

His wife, Caroline (Perlina or Pauline) McLain Howe was left with four children: Henry, eight years old; Frances (Frankie), six years old; Orville, four years old; and Carrie, about three months old, when Marshall died.

Because they had lost their marriage certificate enroute from New York, Caroline was unable to receive a pension for two years. These were hard years for Caroline. She was born on November 12, 1824 into a wealthy family. Her maternal grandfather had married an Indian maiden and they owned a large part of Manhattan Island, New York. Her father, VanRensler McLain, was a son of Uriah McClain who had "taken up land from the government when America was a wilderness." Uriah had two other sons, however, Philander and Adam. Adam went into debt and the brothers signed papers to their property, including land owned by Philander in Swartz Creek, relinquishing the land to pay their brother's debt. "In those days the county could imprison a young man for a small debt," Frances Howe pointed out in her letters.

Caroline lived until March 23, 1905, when she died at the age of 80 and was buried in Flushing, Michigan.

CHILDREN OF MARSHALL B. HOWE AND CAROLINE (McLAIN) HOWE

Henry Albert, born January 13, 1854, New York State.

Frances E. (Frankie), born August 3, 1856, New York State. Frankie went to California but married Charles Fuller and lived in Sparta, Michigan in later years.

ORVILLE MARSHALL BENJAMIN, born December 26, 1858, New York State.

Infant boy, born March 26, 1860, died at birth and buried west of Clio, Michigan.

Carrie, born September 3, 1862, in Michigan.

ORVILLE MARSHALL BENJAMIN HOWE (Author's grandfather)

Born December 26, 1858 in Baldwinville, NY, Cayuga County.
Died January 3, 1944, age 85, in Owosso.
He came to Michigan in 1859 with his parents and went to school in Clio.

Buried in Oak Hill Cemetery, Owosso.

Married Cora Adell Goodnow, October 9, 1880, by Elder Haight in the Methodist Church in Clio.

    Cora Adell Goodnow was born March 26, 1861.

        Mother's name: Evelyn Hoyt

        Father's name: Nelson Goodnow

        Died October 18, 1940, age 79

Orville married a second time in 1942 to Miss Rose Altenberg.

Orville M. Howe was a carpenter by trade and played the violin as a hobby, specializing in old-time music. He was a member of I.O.O.F. at Flint and a member of the Loyal Orangeman's Lodge at Onaway. He lived in Owosso for 15 years before his death. When he died he had 59 grandchildren, 76 great-grandchildren and 1 great-great grandchild.

CHILDREN OF ORVILLE M. AND CORA (GOODNOW) HOWE (11)

Eva married George Bassett in NY and

    (2) Mr. Robinson in Owosso

DEMPSTER MARSHALL HOWE married Estella M. Spencer.

Flora May married Frank Phillip Lytle, Alma.

Edith married Mr. Kerby of Saginaw.

    (2) Mr. Shaffer

    (3) Carl Hartman

Celia married Joe McManus, Flint.

    A granddaughter, Mrs. Joyce Rodgers

    1986 Maplewood Rd., Lennon, MI 48449

Beulah married a Mr. Reed, NY, lived in Portland 1944.

    (2) Mr. Swainson, NY

Margaret married George Rollins (or Rawlins).

Etta married Bill Richardson, lived in Jackson and later, in Owosso.

Cora Adell married Will Wells in Owosso and later was Cora Brown, living in Mt. Clemens.

Orville Bradish married Ruth Yoder, Owosso.

(2) Mary

Earl Nelson born November 28, 1905, Owosso, married Iva Alice DeForest and lived in Raymond, WA, 1944. (Iva lived in So. Bend, WA in 1996.)

Children:

Earl, Jr., born August 19, 1926, Owosso.

Helen Louise, born January 21, 1930, WA; married Mr. Settlemyer, Raymond, WA.

Diane Lynette, born November 24, 1942, WA.

DEMPSTER MARSHALL HOWE (Author's father)

Born January 27, 1883 in West Branch.

Married Estella Maude Spencer, Flint, 1904.

Died January 3, 1968 at age 84.

Buried in Oak Hill Cemetery, Owosso.

Dempster M. Howe lived most of his life in Owosso. At one time he'd worked at Buick in Flint, been a guard at Jackson Prison and been employed in the utilities department of the City of Owosso. He had 14 grandchildren and 20 great-grandchildren when he died.

CHILDREN OF DEMPSTER M. AND ESTELLA (SPENCER) HOWE:

MAY CASTELLA born March 19, 1906, Corunna.

Married John Morrison Beardslee on December 13, 1923. (He died May 21, 1988.)

Eliza Adell born August 5, 1909.

Died June 2, 1918. Buried in Onaway.

Marshall Bradish born March 8, 1912, Pontiac.

Died November 28, 1987, age 75.

Buried in Hillcrest Memorial Gardens, Owosso.

Spent most of his life in Owosso.

Phillip Abraham born April 4, 1915, Onaway.
   Lived in Owosso.
   Married Leona Guentensberger, June 12, 1943.
   Children:
   Jim (Dawn Smith) Howe
   Mrs. Darlene (Thomas) Rench
Dorothy Marjorie born February 27, 1918 in Onaway.
   Married Harold Ordway, July 12, 1936 in Owosso. (He died September 5, 1980.)
   Died on February 10, 1995, age 77.
   Buried in Oak Hill Cemetery, Owosso.
   Children:
   Raymond (Kathy) Ordway, Rohnert Park, CA.
   Richard (Pat) Ordway of Owosso.
   Mrs. Linda (Michael) Bazelides
   Mrs. Jacqueline (Richard) Emberton (Preceded her mother in death.)
Donald Raymond born November 7, 1919 in Owosso.
   Married Flora F. Spencer, March 3, 1944.
   Died December 19, 1990, age 71.
   Buried in Hillcrest Memorial Gardens, Owosso.
   Children:
   Mrs. Janet (Robert) Dougan, Owosso
   Mrs. Connie (Calvin) York, Ft. Lauderdale, FL
   Mrs. Sally (Daniel) Dexter, Owosso
   Douglas D. (Elizabeth) Howe, Lansing
   Thomas R. Howe, Owosso
   Donald was a lifelong resident in Owosso. He was a World War II veteran and owned Howe Janitorial in Owosso until 1975. He retired in 1985 from Buick Motor Division in Flint. He had 14 grandchildren and 2 great-grandchildren at the time of his death.

CHILDREN OF MAY CASTELLA HOWE AND JOHN MORRISON BEARDSLEE

Lillian May born April 17, 1924 in Owosso.
Beverly Ann born December 23, 1929, Lansing.
Joyce Kathryn born September 13, 1931, Lansing.
(See Spencer Family)

NOTES

SAMUEL B. SPENCER

SAMUEL BRADISH SPENCER was the last surviving Civil War veteran in Shiawassee County, according to a report in Owosso Argus Press on the day he died, April 22, 1939. He had taken part in the Memorial Day activities held in Owosso for the past several years and had a large military funeral. He was in the 4th Michigan Infantry, Co. F. while in the service.

"Mr. Spencer was born in New York State on June 28, 1849, the son of Mr. and Mrs. Samuel B. Spencer, Sr. He lived in that state for a number of years during his youth and was one of the first to answer President Lincoln's call to arms in 1860. He was living in Detroit at the time, and was sent to Texas first. While there, camping near San Antonio, the regiment with which he was serving was nearly decimated by drinking stagnant water at a lake that had no inlet or outlet," the Argus Press stated and added, "He served during the entire four years of the War between the States."

He worked as a mason for many years following his return from the Civil War and lived in Flint and Onaway, as well as Corunna and Owosso. Before his retirement, he was employed at the Campbell Cement Products Company in Owosso.

Spencer married Mary E. Willey in January 1872 and they had one daughter, Estelle Maude, who married Dempster Howe. They adopted a son, Samuel Dewey.

Mary died in 1932 and Spencer married a second time in 1933, to Mrs. Cora Diamond, 20 years his junior. In addition to being a member of the G.A.R., he was a member of the Odd Fellows and of the Orangeman's Lodge.

Military rites at his funeral were carried out by a large number of patriotic and civic bodies of Owosso and Corunna. More than 50 members of the Women's Relief Corps attended, as well a many representatives of the American Legion, Veterans of Foreign Wars and Spanish-American War veterans.

"The funeral procession extended for blocks," the Argus Press reported. "And a firing squad fired farewell volleys at the grave. Two buglers sounded "taps", and echoed the final salute from a distance."

SPENCER FAMILY

SAMUEL BRADISH SPENCER (Author's grandfather)
    Born June 28, 1849 in New York State.
    Parents: Mr. and Mrs. Samuel Bradish Spencer, Sr.
    Died April 22, 1939, age 89.
    Buried in Oak Hill Cemetery, Owosso.
    Married Mary Jane Willey, January 14, 1872.
        Born February 28, 1854 in Macomb County.
        Parents: Mr. and Mrs. Charles Willey.
        Two brothers, Minor C. and Elliott A.
        Died February 1932, age 77.
        Buried in Oak Hill Cemetery, Owosso.
        Family lived in Bancroft, Corunna and Owosso.

CHILDREN OF SAMUEL SPENCER and MARY (WILLEY) SPENCER
    Twins: Ollie and Jessie, died of diptheria when three months old.
    Samuel Dewey born August 10, 1899 in Flint.
        Adopted by Spencers when a year old.
        Came to Owosso in 1919.
        Married Florence Safferd, March 29, 1920.
        Children: 5 sons
        Died June 16, 1976, age 76.
        Buried in Hillcrest Memorial Gardens, Owosso.

ESTELLA MAUDE SPENCER (Author's mother)
>Born December 24, 1883 in Bancroft.
>Died April 5, 1969, age 85.
>Buried in Hillcrest Memorial Gardens, Owosso.
>Married Frank Stockinger, 1900.
>Married James Helms, 1902.
>>Son, James Helms, buried in Owosso Cemetery.
>
>Married **DEMPSTER MARSHALL HOWE**, April 1904, in Flint by Justice of the Peace, Mr. Torey.

CHILDREN OF ESTELLA M. SPENCER and DEMPSTER M. HOWE
>**MAY CASTELLA HOWE** born March 19, 1906 in Corunna.
>>Married John Beardslee, December 13, 1923.
>>>He died May 22, 1988. Buried in Chapel Hill Memorial Gardens, Lansing.
>
>Eliza Adell born August 5, 1909 in Flint.
>>Died at age 9 years, June 2, 1918.
>>Buried in Onaway Cemetery.
>
>Marshall Bradish born March 8, 1912 in Pontiac.
>Phillip Abraham born April 4, 1915 in Onaway.
>Dorothy Marjorie born February 27, 1918 in Onaway.
>>Married Harold L. Ordway of Owosso.
>>Died February 10, 1995.
>>Buried Oak Hill Cemetery.
>
>Donald Raymond born November 17, 1920 in Owosso.
>Twin boys, 8-1/4 pounds and 8 pounds, stillborn 1922. Buried in Oak Hill Cemetery, Owosso.

CHILDREN OF MAY CASTELLA HOWE AND JOHN BEARDSLEE
>Lillian May born April, 17, 1924 in Owosso.
>Beverly Ann born December, 23, 1929 in Lansing.
>Joyce Kathryn born September 13, 1931 in Lansing.

NOTES